DISABLED?
DISABLED!
DISABLED

Transitional Poems from the Disability Perspective

DANIEL GARCIA

ARCHWAY
PUBLISHING

Archway Publishing books may be ordered through booksellers or by contacting:

Archway Publishing
1663 Liberty Drive
Bloomington, IN 47403
www.archwaypublishing.com
1 (888) 242-5904

Because of the dynamic nature of the Internet, any web addresses or links contained in this book may have changed since publication and may no longer be valid. The views expressed in this work are solely those of the author and do not necessarily reflect the views of the publisher, and the publisher hereby disclaims any responsibility for them.

Any people depicted in stock imagery provided by Getty Images are models, and such images are being used for illustrative purposes only. Certain stock imagery © Getty Images.

ISBN: 978-1-4808-8772-5 (sc)
ISBN: 978-1-4808-8773-2 (e)

Library of Congress Control Number: 2020902253

Print information available on the last page.

Archway Publishing rev. date: 2/10/2020

To my family, friends, wife and son

Acknowledgment

Thank you to everyone who has supported me, encouraged me and believed in me.

Erika Abbot for my first editing

Brandon Garcia for contributing his art for my bookcover

Arnel Dones for taking my profile picture

Contents

A Bomb

It took an A-bomb
In Hiroshima-Nagasaki,
Burning,
  Mutating,
    Killing,
To end the war
With innocent life.

It took a bomb
In Oklahoma
To take away
Precious children
  O. J. Simpson from the news.
The myth: It can't happen here in the USA.
A bomb.

An Immigrant's Sorrows

I ask forgiveness on this
starry and glowing night
to all those who have loved me
from the distance
or those who have forgotten me
forever.
Because it was all my fault.
Free moments
of the day
I have filled with false joys.,
And every night of dreamy memory
I have filled with nightmares.
Although my heart screams with emotion
in a strange land,
supplications come out
with melancholic voices.
It's like hearing rainy voices
Slowly and clearly.
This is how I implore you
to listen to my laments:
I was able to write long letters—
time made them short,
for stupid time
and lost loves.
I was able to call by phone,
But the money did not come out of my pocket,
and I could have someone

like you by my side
to sing those verses of vagabond love
And feel the brightness of your radiant heart.
The distances
separate us by ten million
tears
from country to country.

Cocaine

I am cocaine.
This is my poem.
I was born innocent.
My mother was a tree
From Machu Picchu.
My father was an Inca,
The proud warrior.
The white men came.
They raped my mother
And stole my father's
Pride,
      Land,
And with his land
         His son.
I was raised by
The white men.
They whitewashed me
From my green nature
To use me for local anesthetic.
Then they discovered that I could be
Used for profit.
Sigmund Freud used me.
The rich ate me in their dessert.
You father drank me in Coca-Cola.
Now I am everywhere,
From
Upper,

Middle,
        Lower
Class.
I am put anywhere
In their body parts
From up to down.
Some like it in the nose,
Others in their nipples,
But I like it in the vagina.
They made me in many forms:
Powder,
        Rock,
                Smoke,
And they name me
Cocaine,
        Crack,
                Ice.
When I am abused,
I drove them crazy.
I made them beg for more.
Then I killed them.
Oh, I am having my bittersweet
Revenge
For what they did
To my mother and father
And me.

Diurnal Ghost

You go out from night to day.
You come, ghost, from my
Nights of pleasure.
I see that you enter into other people.
You surround me with your presence,
But I do not touch you.
Is it you, the one who sings and laughs,
The one who dances with the carnations,
The one who speaks to me with the spring-breeze?
What are you?
My past,
      Present,
            Future?
Who are you?
The one who wakes me up
Saying, "I love you."
And then when I go to bed,
"I do not like you."
Only to return
To you, nocturnal ghost.

Nocturnal Ghost

You wait for me at night
In the most hidden area of my mind.
You throw yourself into my being.
You are looking with passion,
And you find
All the secrets of my life
To fill your life with mine.
I do not know what nights were
The most seductive and ardent,
The most melancholic and joyful,
The most, the most.
In what night was …
That you made me have the urge,
The wishes
To make you real,
To feel my sex,
To rub with pleasure,
But everything seems to be in vain.
The only thing I get out from you,
My ghost,
Is liquid in my hands

From Kid to Man

I used to play with toys,
playing war
or moving little cars
and dreaming with air fighters.
Now I play with
pen and paper,
playing with verbs and nouns,
moving my life far away
and fly with the liberty
of my imagination.
I used to hate girls
and dolls,
hate to be kissed,
give hand,
and hate to make anything
without paying me first.
Now I love girls
and dolls for my loneliness,
love kisses,
feel hand hot and cold,
and love to do things
without money.
I used to say
many bad words at school
and skip classes
without knowing
how wonderful a time

I had lost,
seeing chicks,
making friends,
studying hard
to help people.
Now I'd like to go back
to say "pardon me"
to my life
because
such happiness I didn't have
and lips contacts I have never done.

From Kid to Man

Poem to My Son

I used to see you playing with toys,
Playing with drums and bells
or moving little cars,
dreaming wildly in color.
Now you play with
pen and paper,
playing with colors,
making a reality of your
vivid imagination.
You used to know every
single car that passed by
when we took you out anywhere,
making use of your memories that will be meaningless
but impressive
at the time.
Now you know every color
of the rainbow.
When not using the time for technology,
your mind goes wildly obsessive
in creation mode,
making sure that your life is full
of colors and memories.
You used to be a kid,
Free of obligation and responsibility.
You discovered that crying has
the power to get you anything,

like not eating your veggies
and carrots.
(Thank God for green juice
and Boost.)
Your power of saying no
made my hair turn white without using
any color on me.
Now you are a man,
full of obligations and responsibilities
that the world will demand of you.
You are on a road trip of your own,
discovering new forms of crying,
social justice, equality, and happiness.
Who knew that the white canvas on my beard and
hair
will be used to paint such a masterpiece of a boy
becoming a man?

From Tree to Wood

I am the one who loves you,
But you didn't feel it.
I am the one who spoke to you with the winds,
But you didn't understand.
You sat at my trunk,
And with my branches and leaves
I took the vexatious summer sun.
I was
Your house,
Your place to cry,
Your friend to go to.

When the hand of man
Came to make me
Chair and table,

And yet you passed on my road.
You fail to recognize my fallen leaves,
Poor of you.
They took me for useful things.
That, to me, is not useful.

My Sailor

Oh, sailor, you survived
The Great Depression.
And later you survived
World War II.
You sailed away on the
USS Zellar.
As soon as you landed home
You jumped ship to marry your
Sweetheart girl.
You became a grandpa.
You raised two beautiful
And lovely daughters.
One of them decided
To give you the honorable
Title of zeida.
Who knew?
Who knew that one of your
Grandkids would change everything?
Just like you helped change the world
On the seven seas
With cannon and machine gun.
Dina will and has changed the world
With verbs, nouns, and one smile at the time.
Heck, you even saw the name changing
From Levitz,
To Springer,
To Garcia?

Against all the odds, you came.
You made your bid,
And now you are ready
To set sail one more time
Where mortals have to sail,
To the land called eternity.

I bid you farewell as once more.
The USS Zellar and its crew
Take you to your loved ones.

Farewell.

Guitar

Somebody bought me
Another package.
I felt that they passed me by hand
Like honey passed
From bee to bee.

Waited for two weeks and one day.
For the time being I lurked in the darkness
Of a corner full of shoes and clothes.
Until one day they took me out to the road.

Then listen to my electric cousins.
Later I noticed a chill of people talking.
When all this was over
They began to make terrifying sounds.

A few penetrated the paper,
And I thought it was my end.
Then I felt the caressing, fingers
On my vibrant strings
Like those of angels.
From that moment I knew I was made for you.

I Am a Drop of Water

I am a drop of water.
Many people ask me
Where I can go.
I can go to the big ocean
Or a lake or more simply
To a pond.

Other people want to know
What color I am.

Well, I can be blue-green
Or brown or maybe crystalline.

I don't care where I go or
What color I am.
I only know I am a drop
Of water.

I Am the Wine

I am the wine
That you with elegance
    Take,
        Lift,
            And carry
To your mouth that
Has never been touched
By the passionate lips of man.
With a simple touch
Of your lips,
A drop of me
Falls onto you.
The rest of me goes
To your mouth,
Playing with your tongue,
Savoring and enjoying my
Delicacy.
Penetrating your river of passion,
Cruising the defensive line
Of your heart
Only to encounter
That infinite love of yours.
Meanwhile, the rest of me is in you,
The drop that is running
Softly on your skin,
Exploring your neck,
Adventuring in the darkness

That produces your clothes.
With only a contact with your clothes
I vanish.
In the same time, it vanished your clothes slowly,
As though if I were the acid of love.
Naked you stayed, the same as you were born,
And you will sleep tonight with infinite love
Because the rest of me is in you.

Lady—Apple

I need you, lady, because
You are my sweet apple.
From you, I have taken my first bite.
I call you my apple.
You are red, cheeks and lips,
And each bite, sweet kisses
Like honey just harvested, pure flesh
Of the biggest apple, and the
Most juicy of all the other apples.

Now I have tasted you.
Now only seeds are left,
Seeds that I sowed,
Which I'll care for
Until you become a tree,
And this tree
Becomes a flower,
And the flower
A marvelous mature fruit
That I'll call my apple.

King without Crown

They blame me
For not having
A crown and kingdom,

Crown of fragrant body
And absent king.
You were born among roses
White and red.
People took from the golden honey.
They bathe you in the diamond river.

Crown of night
Without star
In your splendid
Darkness,
You fail to see
Your reflection in time.

Oh, crown of spring,
In the morning
You went on your own,
So jovial and carefree.
Everyone desired you,
But nobody deserves you.

Crown of winter,
In a distant balcony
Tears were falling

As you listened
To my war cry.

After so many wars
To crown me
I made her out of thorns,
And you sat there without
Seeing my blood on the
Road to my throne.

A Valentine Chocolate

I am dark and sweet as sin.
I am indulgent of your body.
You know that you crave me.
Like cacao and milk
I tempt your tongue.
I swim in your saliva,
And you make sure
You swallow it all.
I seduce your mind
Until you are mine,
Driving you crazy.
It is what I was made for.
I know I can be merciless,
And I won't let you escape.
You may break me to pieces,
But in the end
I am whole.
I am best when combining with
Orange,
    Strawberry
And hot chili pepper.
They are all fun to try.
You tried me
In any form
Tootsie Roll,
Cake,
And spicy, warm, wet tamale.

I have even a special day
Where you want me the most.
I said enough
For me to get you in.
Now it is time for action,
For ecstasy. Not even the goddess
Can refuse me
Because I am a heavenly delight.
I am chocolate for your life.

Plastic Island, Graveyard of Conveniences

I am a wounded bird
Who tries to fly to
The eternal blue sky
And look from above.
The whole thing is tiny,
That it is.
But I'm hurt.
How I would like to fly again
Without the plastic in my neck.
The sky was ours.
Before came that destructive being,
Enemy of all the animals,
Self-serving and conscious
Creator of the plastic island
For their own convenience.
Before, it was the land,
After, the sea,
Now, the sky.
We were given the sky
To be free of the
Gravity.
Now who will heal me?
People?
Not!
Once they find me

They will give their excuses:
"But he is suffering!"
They will become my final solution
And meet my end.

Question

What would you like to say?

I hate you,
I hate you!
I hate you?

Or

I love you,
I love you!
I love you?

Or maybe

Love-war

War-love.

It likes to say
Nothing to the nothing.

It is like a person who looks
At the windows
To get free answers
Because all the answers
Are in you.

So close to your
Eyes,
      Mind,
Soul.
There will never be an answer
If you don't take a step away.

Romancing Liar

Forgive me.
Forgive me if I had been lying
To you.
Forgive me if I had done it
To hurt you,
If I had lost the best part of my life,
If I recognized the love and care
You were giving me.
Forgive me
If I told you that
I don't care for you anymore
Because I am lying.
Again,
Please forgive me.

Telling You the Ways
I Miss You

How many verses have I written for you?
And you have not read them.
How many love letters and supplications
I have sent you,
And you have not answered me.
How I love those wet red lips
That once kissed me before,
Your hands that once caressed me,
My face,
My chest,
My innermost being,
Your free hair playing with the wind.
I miss the softness of your voice
That penetrated my ears,
Like whispers of the sea.
Your eyes looked like crystal-clear blue water.
How can I forget that distant starry night
When you supported your head
And kissed you in the calm sea.
My hands were looking for your face,
My eyes were looking for your curves
And my body was touching your body.
Sometimes I found you in places with
Stars without light and restless seas.
Love, you were indeed my hope,
My new light.

You were the key to my life.
You were daylight.

Now I'm afraid to sleep between cold sheets,
Of not seeing your face on my pillow,
And not smelling the perfumes
That so many men have conquered.
Lonely dreams will return
In my eternal paradise.
They will enter with your face
Next to mine,
Touching your skin with fire,
And feeling your heart beating.
Upon awakening, everything vanishes.
You open doors and windows.
You open the hidden treasure of centuries
Given by the goddess Venus
To men of heart
To change
The world of burial and steel,
To reality and fantasy,
Happiness and peace.

The Beach

Let me be one who
Guides,
      Speaks,
           Feels.
Let me be the
Light,
      Sound,
           Warm touch.
Let me be the
Sun,
      Wave,
           Sand,
Let me the beach.

The Judgement

I do not judge God or the devil
For possessing those powers
Of great magnitude.
They watch us
Day and night,
One in heaven,
Another underground.

I do not judge my mother or father
For taking me to the right path
Screaming and caressing.
Thus I was forming my own being.

I do not judge my next being.
I do not judge the poor
For being poor.
I do not judge the rich
Whose money they work for,
Some by profiting,
Others by luck.

I judge humanity
For not finding
Common ground,
But again
It would not be human.

The Twin Towers

"Fire, fire!"
It is all over me.

"Fire, fire."
Everyone went out.
Look up, down.
side to side.

Soon enough
police,
        firefighters,
                    reporters,
surrounded the buildings.

They went into the mouth of hell,
and they never came back
the same.

Made the twin torchlights
Aiming at heaven
Ever so much brighter
To the open sky.

The Two Cups of Life
The Story of American Politics Made Simple

Once upon a time,
there were two empty cups
sitting side by side.
Both of them were thirsty.
Down came the rain,
and they equally got half of the liquid of life.
"Hi, I am Half Full," said the first cup.
"Hi, I am Half Empty," said the second cup.
"Nice to meet you."
One day Half Empty wasn't feeling well.
"Is everything all right?" said Half Full.
"I am feeling lonely," said Half Empty.
"I am going to give you
my first drop of friendship,"
said Half Full,
"So that you can become Half Fuller."
They became good friends.
"I feel that the sun is boiling my water,"
said Half Empty.
"Don't worry.
I'll give you more of my water,"
said Half Full.
"I feel very positive that the rain will come."

"I'm not satisfied with the amount of rain
that landed in my cup,"

said Half Empty.
"Okay, let me give you half of mine,"
Said Half Full.
"But how can you give me your Half Full?"
said Half Empty.
"Are you not concerned about the
liquid of life in your cup?"
"No," said Half Full.
"Why?" said Half Empty.
With high optimism Half Full said,
"Because your cup will always
be full of our water, yours and mine."

What Dick and Jane Forgot to Say

You don't remember me,
but
I remember you,
      standing,
   walking,
socializing.
You don't know me,
but
I know you,
the slaver,
   baby stealer,
      war maker,
   disabled maker,
love maker.
Am I being too harsh on you?
Oh, but
I know that you have been harsher on us.
Putting us in the rehab institution
where your sister was raped
while in a coma
and
your brother,
covered in war medals,
can't find a job.
Until he found the only job

that he was trained
to do well was
killing
himself.
Or
your daughter being sterilized
because you thought she could not
take care of her baby.
Abandoning your wife
after you found out
she was quadriplegic.
You don't remember me
before infamous Auschwitz.
There were institutions of death,
merciful death,
more death,
but
I remember you,
concentration camp,
final solution,
the Holocaust,
Ten million people killed.
They started with me,
cerebral palsy,
     mental retardation,
spinal cord injury,
but
they ended with you,
          gays,
       Jews,

European melting pots.
Remember,
whatever happens to me
could happen to you.

Disability Relationship at School

You are the light of day
That illuminates my heart.
You are the rose
I cut with love.
Why do you now leave me
When I need you the most?
It is as if I have fallen into a pit
Without being able to hold on to you.
Without you, I cannot get out whole.
When I approach you
You move away from me.
Do you not know how to treat me?
Tell me without fear,
Have I been bad for you?
Have I mistreated your feelings?
Please, tell me
So I may not be
Ignorant throughout my life.
It does not matter how far you strayed.
I want you to know
I will always be proud of having you.
I want you to think
The light that once illuminated my life
Will no longer be you,

And my incomplete body that came out
Of the pit will not be the same.
But I always remember the lessons
And not the last friend I will have.

Mermaid

I remember that night.
We were watching
the infinite blue sea
As if it were today.
Yes, I remember that rock
we sat on
to see the twilight of eternity.
We sat there
to hear the roar of the waves crashing
and the supplications of the seagulls.
While I was contemplating your hair
long and beautiful,
your concentrated and fixed eyes,
the enjoyment of your lips as I kissed you.
I remember being immobile when listening to
those beautiful songs of your wandering voice.
As you sang my sadness away,
the cool wind settled down.
Mermaid, the day I die, I want you to sing
to kids.
I want you to write "I love you"
in the water.
My soul will be hidden
like a treasure chest
never to be found.

Homelessness

Was walking on my long, dusty route of bitterness,
Walking at night, sleeping during the day,
Because the sun did not belong to me.
Just as things came and went
To my aching, tired heart,
I arrived at a house, and I was hungry.
A soft and kind voice attended me.
Someone with heavenly eyes saw me.
Hairs of wheat amazed me.
She opened the door of her heart
And invited me to try her infinite body she offered me.
Her mouth was a glass of red wine.
Her skin of meringues gave to me.
After having savored the pleasures,
She provided her delicate back
To write a piece of my bitter life on it,
And sweetness became my soul.

Friend

Friend, I thank you with all my soul
Because you are understanding and adorable.
You are a star in the glow of night,
And you shine like the colors of the rainbow.

When you wear a dress, you look more beautiful
That a newly blooming rose.

Friend, when you sit down with someone,
Do not let your shyness take hold of you
Because maybe that someone who is there
Needs to be understood.

When you are sad, smile, because a smile of yours
Is enough to smile at the world, and the world will
Smile at you.

If you have doubts
Or someone did you wrong,
Do not stop going to your friends.
When they are not there,
Do not think that you are alone
Because there is something,
And it will find you.
Friend, there are doors in life.
Some of these doors
Are happiness, love, maturity, faith.

Teacher

You educate with your energies and patience.
You work for all children.

You are the second mother.
This school is my second home,
And my room is solitude.
Education, hope to get ahead,

I thank you for your advice,
Which is like a path that must be followed.

You are like a rose,
And with your scent you perfume each child
You educate day after day.

Teacher, you are the tree of ripe fruit.
You are the white dove that brings peace and
wisdom
To my existence. You are the light that never
goes out,
You who taught me to make poems with a pencil
and sheet.

Oh! Teacher, I have so many memories of you.
I'm going to teach my children how you taught me,
With patience, joy, wisdom, and love.

Suicidal Nation

You called the collapsing
Of my lungs
        A hoax,
Fake news,
        Lying fact,
Like you needed an excuse
To go drilling
For more oil and gold.
You made improvements
After you realized that
You were too lazy to pick up
Your own trash
In your own
                    Rivers,
            Lakes,
        Oceans.
You created the
Environmental Protection Agency.
You thought if the trash is not
There any more,
Everything will be all right.
Wrong, that was your test
Of how much you love
                    Clean water,
            Food,
        Air.
Obviously, you did

Until
Your greed became president,
Your absurdity became fact,
Your survival became suicidal.
If tree leaves were the shape of
Paper money,
You would understand that
Your bank account is on fire.
The Amazon and African jungles
Are my lungs.
Once my lungs are not there
You will find a way to capitalize air
Like you are doing with water.
That is a suicidal nation for you.

Dumpster

You can find me anywhere
Because I am essential
But not wanted.
Inside,
You can find
Unwanted things
Like broken chairs,
Broken pieces of memory,
Broken bodies.
In front,
Residue can be found
Of things that people
Would like you to keep.
Behind,
Laying on the ground,
A woman
Cries
Naked,
Discarded of her
Humanity.
I said,
"I am essential
But not wanted."

Holocaust

My name is Holocaust.
The Nazis made my name in ashes
From the flesh of Jews, gypsies, and "useless eaters."

I became known by many
as humanity's worst nightmare
and a field of dreams
for humanity's worst masochists.

The less you speak about me
the stronger I become.
The sooner you forget about me
the faster I will arrive to steal
your last breath
again.

My name is Holocaust,
And you better forget me not
as I rest asleep
with the souls and ashes
of millions.

I promise you
that if you visit me
in my killing fields
where I somberly sleep,
I will hold on, killing you again.

Printed in the United States
By Bookmasters